Original title:
Reflections in the Celestial Abyss

Author: Swan Charm
ISBN HARDBACK: 978-1-80561-450-0
ISBN PAPERBACK: 978-1-80561-475-3

Twinkling Echoes in the Cosmic Canvas

Stars are scattered bright and wide,
In the velvet of the night.
Echoes from the past collide,
Painting dreams in silver light.

Galaxies dance in silent grace,
Spirals twirling, lost in flight.
Time stands still in this vast space,
Whispers woven, soft and light.

Nebulas bloom in colors bold,
Cradling secrets yet untold.
Each twinkle is a story old,
In this canvas, life unfolds.

Comets trace their fleeting path,
Leaving traces of their fire.
In the darkness, laughter's wrath,
Fueling sparks of deep desire.

In every beat of cosmic song,
We find a thread that binds us near.
Together where we all belong,
In cosmic echoes, hearts hold dear.

The Night's Caress Through Cosmic Eyes

Beneath the blanket of the night,
Soft shadows dance, a gentle sway.
Stars awaken in their light,
Guiding dreams that drift away.

Moonbeams weave through branches bare,
A silver touch on quiet ground.
In this hush, we feel the air,
Magic whispers all around.

The universe holds tales untold,
In every spark, a story lies.
Secrets of the brave and bold,
Reflected in the cosmic skies.

Each heartbeat syncs with starlit flow,
In the embrace of night's soft breath.
Together with the night we grow,
In shadows, we find life in death.

Eyes to the heavens, dreams take flight,
The night's caress in whispers sweet.
Boundless love in endless night,
In cosmic dance, our souls repeat.

Luminous Thoughts in Lunar Pools

In stillness of the night, it gleams,
Reflections dance on silent streams.
Whispers of the moonlight glide,
Where dreams and gentle waters ride.

Thoughts ablaze in silver glow,
Secrets of the deep below.
Cradled by the tides of time,
Each ripple sings a soft, sweet rhyme.

Hours pass like fleeting breath,
Embraced by the allure of depth.
I wander through this radiant veil,
With each pulse, hear the universe's tale.

A symphony of stars align,
Their echoes linger like fine wine.
In lunar pools, I find my peace,
As thoughts entwine and never cease.

Translucent moments softly sway,
Guiding hearts along their way.
In the night's embrace, I yearn,
For luminous thoughts, forever turned.

The Abyss Stares Back with Glitter

In shadows deep where silence dwells,
The abyss calls with ancient spells.
Eyes like lanterns pierce the night,
Revealing truths that cloak the light.

Glittering paths through darkness weave,
A journey few would dare conceive.
Secrets held in trembling hands,
Beneath the void where starlight lands.

Every heartbeat echoes low,
As fear and wonder start to grow.
In depths of black, I face my fate,
The abyss grins, it's never late.

In shimmering fear, I lose my way,
A dance with doubt, a solemn play.
Yet in the gloom, a spark ignites,
Guiding souls through endless nights.

The abyss reflects my own despair,
Yet in its gaze, I find the rare.
With glitter bright, I challenge dark,
Transforming shadows into spark.

Transcendence in the Midnight Waters

Through midnight waters, I shall drift,
Where stars above are nature's gift.
A current pulls, so soft, so sweet,
Carrying me where spirits meet.

Transcendence calls in waves so clear,
The echoing whispers, truly near.
In depths of blue, I shed my skin,
Letting go of what has been.

Ripples of time flow ever on,
Each moment dances, gently drawn.
An endless stretch of liquid grace,
In midnight's arms, I find my place.

Underneath the silver dome,
Lost in the tides, I feel at home.
In the calming embrace of night,
Transcendence grants my soul its flight.

Awash with dreams of past and chance,
In waters deep, I learn to dance.
A union found beneath the stars,
In midnight waters, we're never far.

Voyages Through Celestial Ripples

On cosmic tides, my spirit sails,
Through endless realms where wonder hails.
Celestial ripples guide my course,
In starlit paths, I find my force.

Each wave a story, each pulse a song,
An ancient dance where souls belong.
Through nebulae, I journey wide,
In whispered paths where dreams abide.

Galactic whispers lead the way,
In twilight's glow, I drift and sway.
The universe, a breathing dome,
In every star, I find my home.

With every turn, new worlds unfold,
Eternal truths in stardust told.
Voyages through time and space,
Each rippling moment, an endless grace.

As comets rush and galaxies spin,
The vastness beckons me within.
Through celestial ripples, I find the call,
In cosmic seas, I am part of all.

Navigating the Cosmic Tides Within

Through stardust paths we glide,
Inward to the heart's deep core,
Whispers of the universe wide,
Only echoes of ancient lore.

Celestial maps we trace,
In silence where constellations dwell,
Orbs of light in endless space,
Guiding us through shadows' spell.

Emotions like comets flare,
Sailing forth on dreams so bright,
Every heartbeat, every prayer,
Resonates with cosmic light.

Waves of time gently flow,
In the depths where stars collide,
In our souls, the secrets grow,
As we ride the cosmic tide.

In this journey of the mind,
We awaken the endless night,
Truth and wonder intertwined,
Navigating our inner light.

Twinkling Memories in Galactic Waters

In the depths of time so clear,
Memories shimmer, soft and bright,
Drifting through the cosmic sphere,
Twinkling like stars in the night.

Echoes of laughter resound,
Ripples on a silver stream,
In celestial realms profound,
We find fragments of a dream.

Every star a tale to share,
Whispers of love from afar,
Drifting on the cosmic air,
Each a timeless shining star.

Galactic waves our hearts embrace,
Carrying stories that we've spun,
In the vastness, we find our place,
Twinkling memories, never done.

Through the cosmos, we will sail,
On waters vast and full of grace,
Tracing every sweet detail,
In the galaxy's warm embrace.

Night's Embrace in a Horizon of Stars

Underneath the starlit veil,
Night entwines us, soft and dear,
In its arms, we shall not fail,
Finding solace, free from fear.

The horizon blooms with light,
Stars like blossoms in the black,
Guiding dreams that take their flight,
As we wander, we turn back.

Moments shared beneath the sky,
Whispers hid in shadows deep,
Though the world may pass us by,
In this embrace, our secrets keep.

Every sparkle tells a tale,
Of the heart's uncharted seas,
In the night, our hopes set sail,
Carried forth on gentle breeze.

In the silence, we discover,
Connections that our souls ignite,
Boundless beauty, like no other,
In night's embrace, we find our light.

Ethereal Flames in the Dark Expanse

In the dark, a flicker grows,
Ethereal flames that dance and sway,
In the void where silence flows,
Guardians of the night and day.

Each ember holds a story bright,
Woven in the threads of time,
Glowing softly, pure delight,
Burning bright in space's rhyme.

A universe of dreams revealed,
In the shadows, warmth ignites,
Through the darkness, fate is sealed,
Eternal light through endless nights.

As we chase these fiery sparks,
With every breath, creation starts,
Illuminating cosmic arcs,
Guiding our wandering hearts.

In the dark, where dreams expand,
These flames will light our way anew,
Together, hand in hand we'll stand,
In the expanse, both brave and true.

Celestial Musings of the Night

The moon glows soft and bright,
Whispers secrets, then takes flight.
Stars are scattered like a dream,
In the stillness, silence beams.

Night is draped in velvet dark,
Each twinkle holds a tiny spark.
Winds carry tales from afar,
Guided by the evening star.

Dreamers dwell in shadowed light,
Chasing phantoms of the night.
Thoughts in rhythm softly flow,
Painting worlds where wishes grow.

Ethereal sounds begin to rise,
Singing lullabies to the skies.
In the quiet, hearts take wing,
To the cosmos, spirits cling.

In this realm where dreams unite,
Time dissolves in gentle flight.
Celestial musings softly weave,
A tapestry of stars we leave.

The Depths of Cosmic Mirrors

Reflections dance upon the sea,
Galaxies swirl, wild and free.
Each ripple holds a hidden gaze,
In dreams, we wander endless maze.

Time and space begin to blend,
In the depths, realities bend.
Mirrors shine with truths untold,
Whispers of the brave and bold.

Stars emerge from stardust's breath,
Carving paths through life and death.
In the void, we find our place,
Mapping out the cosmic space.

Visions shimmer, fade, and glint,
In the shadows where we hint.
Deeper meanings wake our souls,
In the weave, we find our roles.

From these depths, our spirits soar,
Chasing echoes, wanting more.
In the cosmic dance we find,
A universe that's intertwined.

Starlit Reveries of the Heart

In the quiet of the night,
Hearts ignite with starlit light.
Each pulse sings a gentle tune,
Beneath the watchful silver moon.

Memories drift on whispered breeze,
Carried far through ancient trees.
Every glance, a timeless spark,
Illuminating shadows dark.

Wishes wrapped in soft embrace,
Tracing paths in empty space.
With each breath, a dream takes flight,
Guided by the stars so bright.

Stories shared beneath the sky,
Laughter dances, spirits fly.
In starlit reveries, we find,
The universe within our mind.

Together in the night we roam,
Each heartbeat echoes, feels like home.
With every star, a tale is spun,
In this realm, we are all one.

Infinities Cradled in Silence

In the hush of a cosmic night,
Endless wonders take their flight.
Galaxies spin in tranquil dance,
Whispers fading, lost in chance.

Silence wraps the universe tight,
Cradling secrets, pure delight.
In the void, we hear the call,
Echoes of the great, the small.

Stars ignite in fleeting grace,
Transcending time, they leave no trace.
Infinities weave through the dark,
Each moment, a fragile spark.

As constellations brush the sky,
Dreamers in their realms may fly.
Cradled deep within the sound,
In silent depths, we are found.

With every heartbeat, we connect,
Infinities we won't neglect.
Embrace the calm, the still embrace,
In silence, find our destined place.

Gazing Into Infinity's Tender Depths

In whispers soft, the stars ignite,
Each sparkle blooms, a fleeting sight.
A dance of light in velvet skies,
Where dreams are born and silence flies.

Through endless voids, I wander free,
With every step, a new decree.
Galaxies swirl, their secrets kept,
In tender depths where shadows wept.

Cosmic tides pull at my core,
As timeless echoes gently score.
I reach for sparks, they drift away,
In stillness found, I long to stay.

The heart expands, the voids unite,
A tapestry of dark and light.
In each soft pulse, a prayer spun,
Embracing all, we are as one.

Gazing deep, the soul reflects,
In the fine weave, each thought connects.
Infinity whispers in my ear,
A boundless love, forever near.

The Universe in a Cup of Starlight

A porcelain dream, still and bright,
Filled with the glow of endless night.
Each sip reveals a world apart,
The cosmos stirs within my heart.

Galaxies swirl in gentle brew,
A fragrant dance of silver hue.
Constellations sparkle, intertwine,
In every drop, the stars align.

With trembling hands, I hold the sky,
As countless worlds begin to sigh.
The universe, within my reach,
In every taste, it finds its speech.

Planets drift like leaves in air,
Each moment crafted with such care.
A cosmic journey in my cup,
I raise it high, I drink it up.

In starlit sips, I find my place,
A galaxy wrapped in quiet grace.
The universe whispers, soft and sweet,
In this small world, my heart's retreat.

Chasing Shadows Across Celestial Oceans

On waves of light, I sail the night,
Chasing shadows, a fleeting sight.
With every breath, a cosmic dance,
The stars invite my heart's romance.

Celestial tides shift and sway,
Guiding souls who've lost their way.
In vastness wrapped, the echoes play,
As dreams unfurl at break of day.

Beneath the glow of twilight's veil,
I follow trails of starlit sail.
The universe hums a haunting tune,
As shadows weave beneath the moon.

Each surge of light, a whispered prayer,
Connecting hearts that linger there.
In oceans deep, I find my fate,
In timeless embrace, I contemplate.

With silent grace, I wander free,
In endless search of what will be.
Chasing shadows, a brave pursuit,
In cosmic realms, my heart takes root.

Palettes of Light in the Cosmic Twilight

Colors bleed across the night,
With every brush, the stars alight.
In cosmic hues, the heavens dance,
A painter's dream, a timeless chance.

With every stroke, the void will sing,
As shadows stretch on whispered wing.
In twilight's grasp, the canvas grows,
Where space and time, a river flows.

Brush of starlight, tint of dreams,
Colorful whispers, soft moonbeams.
A palette drawn from deep within,
The art of love, where I begin.

Golden trails of comet's flight,
Illuminate the softest night.
In gentle flicks, creation reigns,
As beauty basks in its domains.

In luminous waves, I find my place,
A stroke of hope, a breath of grace.
In cosmic twilight, colors beam,
Together woven, our shared dream.

Whispers of Starlit Depths

In the quiet of the night,
Stars gather in a dance,
Whispers float on gentle winds,
Calling dreams to take a chance.

A galaxy of secrets,
Hidden in cosmic lace,
The moonlight bathes the world,
In its tender, glowing embrace.

Fading echoes of the past,
Twinkling like shimmering dew,
Each twinkling light a story,
A journey weaved anew.

In the heart of every spark,
A universe does bloom,
Beyond the night's soft shadow,
Lies the promise of a dawn.

So lay your cares to rest,
And let your spirit soar,
For the starlit depths await,
With adventures to explore.

Echoes Beneath the Cosmic Veil

Underneath the endless sky,
Whispers blend with silent grace,
A tapestry of wonders,
Woven within time and space.

Starry eyes gaze down upon,
The dreams we weave at night,
Guiding us through shadows,
To realms of brilliant light.

Through the void, a question asked,
What lies beyond the stars?
A journey etched in stardust,
Etched upon our hearts.

In the echoes of the past,
Ancient stories interlace,
Celestial songs enshrouded,
In the night's warm embrace.

So let us heed the whispers,
That flutter through the dark,
Beneath the cosmic veil,
Our spirits find their spark.

Dreams Adrift in the Infinite Sea

On the waves of endless night,
Dreams set sail beside the moon,
Drifting softly through the stars,
To a celestial tune.

Each ripple tells a story,
Of wonders yet to be,
A voyage through the cosmos,
In a world that's wild and free.

Caught between the tides of time,
We dance on the ocean's crest,
With the universe as our guide,
Our spirits feel at rest.

The horizon calls us forward,
To realms beyond our sight,
Where wishes are like starlight,
And every dream takes flight.

So raise your sails to the heavens,
Let your heart drift and roam,
For in the infinite sea,
All dreams will find their home.

Celestial Shadows on Still Waters

Beneath the stars, the waters gleam,
Reflections of a tranquil night,
Celestial shadows softly play,
In the embrace of silver light.

A whisper of the cosmos,
Riding on the surface smooth,
The moon guides every ripple,
With its gentle, soothing groove.

Silence reigns in this moment,
Ink-black sky meets liquid hue,
Together weaving memories,
Of worlds both old and new.

Each star a fleeting heartbeat,
A promise of what's to be,
In the calm of endless waters,
We find our destiny.

So let the night enfold you,
In its cool and calming shade,
For in celestial shadows,
Our brightest dreams are made.

Celestial Currents of Thought

In silence whispers the night,
Dreams like comets take flight.
Thoughts drift on a cosmic breeze,
Floating like leaves on ancient trees.

Stars twinkle with secrets unsaid,
Illuminating paths where minds have tread.
Through galaxies where visions soar,
Waves of wonder evermore.

Underneath the vast expanse,
Ideas dance in a cosmic trance.
Each pulse an echo, every sigh,
An urge to question, to wonder why.

Mind's journey through space and time,
Exploring the depths in rhythmic rhyme.
A tapestry woven with threads of belief,
Finding solace in celestial relief.

So let thoughts wander, unconfined,
In the currents of the starry mind.
For every spark that ignites the night,
Holds a universe of hidden light.

Luminous Tide of Secret Thoughts

A tide of whispers, soft and bright,
Secrets in shadows find their light.
Thoughts like waves caress the shore,
Carrying dreams from deep, evermore.

In the depths where silence dwells,
Stories weave like intricate spells.
Beneath the surface, pulses churn,
To the rhythm of hearts that yearn.

Captive reflections dance and play,
Brightening the night into day.
Hidden treasures of the mind,
Glimmering, waiting to be unlined.

With every ebb, a tale unfolds,
A symphony of the quiet, bold.
Echoes of what's felt but unsaid,
In the luminous tide, softly spread.

So let your thoughts sail, brave and free,
On waves of light through the cosmic sea.
For every secret you hold so dear,
Holds the power to draw you near.

The Abyss Within the Stars

In the void where silence breathes,
Galaxies hide what our soul weaves.
A canvas of dreams stretched wide,
Where shadows of the past abide.

Lost within the starry depth,
We question the life we have kept.
Each flicker, a memory of grace,
Cradled in the night's embrace.

Diving into the cosmic sea,
To find what's always been within me.
The light and dark in eternal dance,
Both part and whole, a timeless chance.

With every wish cast into night,
The abyss cradles our hidden light.
In the quiet, we learn to see,
That stars reflect our longing to be.

Reach into the darkness, hold it tight,
For there in the shadows lives the light.
The abyss whispers secrets profound,
In its depths, true peace is found.

Cosmic Shadows and Ethereal Glows

In a dance of shadows, stars collide,
Ethereal glows where dreams reside.
Softly tracing the edges of night,
Where darkness and hope intertwine in light.

Cosmic whispers carry a tune,
Songs that rise with the silver moon.
Each note a fragment of timeless lore,
Resonating deep, forevermore.

Through the ether, muted and bright,
Shadows reveal the unseen flight.
Spectral glimmers across the void,
A tapestry of creation enjoyed.

In silence we gather what's lost,
Navigating the stars, counting the cost.
For every shadow there lies a glow,
A reminder of paths we yearn to know.

So let us dwell in these realms unknown,
Where shadows are seeds that have been sown.
In the cosmic ballet, together we flow,
Embracing both darkness and ethereal glow.

Pilgrims of the Night Sky

Beneath the stars we wander free,
With dreams that dance like light at sea.
Guided by the moon's soft glow,
We seek the paths that night will show.

In silence, whispers fill the air,
Each heartbeat echoes a quiet prayer.
The universe unfolds its arms,
Embracing us with cosmic charms.

Our souls alight with stardust dreams,
Where nothing is as simple as it seems.
Through shimmering worlds, we tread with care,
Finding solace in wonders rare.

The constellations call our names,
In their embrace, we play with flames.
What stories do they wish to share?
A cosmic tale of love laid bare.

As dawn approaches, we must depart,
Yet night's sweet memory stays in our heart.
Pilgrims we are of the night sky,
Forever longing, forever high.

Luminescent Trails in the Darkness

A flicker in the void appears,
Guiding us through our hidden fears.
Threads of light weave through the black,
Creating paths we never lack.

Each glow a tale of what has been,
In the hush where dreams are seen.
Luminous echoes dance and play,
Leading us gently on our way.

Through shadows deep, our spirits soar,
With every step, we seek for more.
Stars twinkle like forgotten love,
Radiant whispers from above.

In the darkness, hearts ignite,
Finding warmth in the depth of night.
These luminescent trails we trace,
Carve our journey through time and space.

As dawn embraces the day's return,
In every heart, a spark will burn.
Though trails may fade as light breaks free,
The dark remains a part of me.

Echoes in the Quiet Expanse

In the vastness, silence reigns,
Where echoes linger, love remains.
Gentle whispers through the void,
Each breath a bond that can't be destroyed.

Time unfolds in delicate flow,
Carving paths where feelings grow.
In the space where we both reside,
Two souls intertwined, side by side.

The cosmos hums a gentle tune,
Beneath a watchful silver moon.
Each heartbeat sings a song of peace,
In the quiet, our worries cease.

Moments linger like a sweet refrain,
In the expanse, our love remains.
Echoes dance, a delicate art,
A symphony played in every heart.

As stars align in perfect grace,
We trace our dreams in endless space.
In the quiet, we shall find,
The echoes of our hearts aligned.

Ripples of Time Across the Universe

Waves of time ripple through the night,
Carrying whispers of lost delight.
Each second flows like rivers wide,
A tapestry where memories reside.

Across the cosmos, moments weave,
Dreams unravel in time's reprieve.
Stars flicker with the tales they tell,
Of worlds forgotten, under their spell.

Distant galaxies sing a tune,
Of light years journeyed, beneath the moon.
Every heartbeat, a pulse in time,
Echoed in rhythms, soft and sublime.

In this dance of cosmic grace,
We find our place in time and space.
Ripples spread, connecting skies,
Where every moment dares to rise.

As the universe spins on its wheel,
With each new dawn, our dreams reveal.
Ripples of time, forever in flight,
Guiding us through the endless night.

Light of Distant Worlds Reflected

Stars sparkle like diamonds bright,
Revealing tales of cosmic flight.
Galaxies swirl in a dance divine,
Each flicker tells of space and time.

In voids where silence deeply dwells,
Echoes weave their timeless spells.
Light years drift in ethereal grace,
Inspiring wonders, we embrace.

Planets whisper of ancient lore,
Guardians of secrets evermore.
Nebulas bloom with vibrant hues,
Under the cosmos, dreams infuse.

Comets blaze, a fleeting spark,
Illuminating shadows dark.
From distant realms, their stories stream,
In starlit paths, we find our dream.

Through the tapestry of night's embrace,
We glimpse the heart of time and space.
As light cascades from afar,
We gather wishes on a star.

Voyage Through Celestial Waters

Sailing through endless cosmic seas,
Riding currents of stardust breeze.
Waves of light crash upon the shore,
Of mysteries held in the universe's core.

Celestial boats with sails of fire,
Charting paths that never tire.
Constellations guide our quest,
Each star a compass, we are blessed.

In the depths where silence reigns,
Discoveries swim through cosmic chains.
Galactic tides pull us near,
To worlds unknown, beyond the sphere.

Reflections shimmer on the night's skin,
A dance of light where dreams begin.
Explorers of the astral tide,
In the heart of the void, we abide.

With every wave, a new tale unfolds,
In the ocean of stars, adventure bold.
Together we drift, a celestial team,
Navigating the cosmos, we dare to dream.

Quietude in the Nebulous Night

In shadows soft, where silence sighs,
Dreams take flight 'neath velvet skies.
Whispers of stars in gentle light,
Cloak the universe in tender night.

Nebulas cradle secrets untold,
In their embrace, we feel the old.
Mysteries swirl in colors bright,
In the hush of the cosmos' night.

Stillness reigns in the dark expanse,
In quietude, we find our chance.
To listen deep to cosmic flows,
As the universe softly glows.

Galaxies breathe with tranquil grace,
Painting stories in the space.
Within the calm, our spirits rise,
Carried onward by the skies.

Each moment cherished, every breath deep,
In the heart of silence, we are steeped.
From cosmic whispers, understanding grows,
In the gentle night, tranquility flows.

Whispers of the Galactic Sea

Waves of starlight touch the shore,
Secrets carried forevermore.
Whispers echo in the night,
Tales of wonder, pure delight.

In the depths of the cosmic tide,
Universes swirl, collide, and glide.
Voices call from beyond the dark,
Igniting passions, a celestial spark.

Constellations weave their song,
A harmony where we belong.
As comets dance through the air,
Each moment filled with love and care.

Oceans of stars beneath our feet,
A journey that feels so sweet.
With galaxies as our guide,
In this adventure, we abide.

Through the cosmic currents, we roam,
Finding in the vastness, a home.
Together we sail, hearts aglow,
In whispers of wonder, the stars bestow.

Fractals of Time in Twilight

In twilight whispers, shadows play,
The fractals dance, then drift away.
Moments bend in silent streams,
Fragile threads of fading dreams.

A universe of shifting light,
Patterns woven, day to night.
Memory's touch, so faint yet bright,
A tapestry of endless flight.

Time unravels, secrets told,
In every curve, a hint of gold.
The twilight glows with ancient grace,
In fractals vast, we find our place.

Embrace the echoes soft and true,
In twilight's arms, we start anew.
Each heartbeat marks a fleeting phase,
In fractured light, the past stays.

So gather round, let shadows weave,
A twilight dream we still believe.
In fractals spun with tender care,
We hold the time we long to share.

The Heartbeat of Distant Galaxies

In cosmic depths, a heartbeat drifts,
Across the void, through starlit rifts.
Galaxies pulse with ancient sound,
A rhythm lost yet ever found.

Waves of light in colors swirl,
In massive orbs, the heavens twirl.
Each star a tale of time and space,
With vibrant echoes, we embrace.

Beyond the nebulae so grand,
The music flows from a timeless hand.
Filling the silence, an ageless tune,
In the vast night, under a silver moon.

Whispers of worlds long gone,
In every pulse, a sage's song.
The heartbeat of galaxies far and wide,
Unites us all in the cosmic tide.

Together we roam the stellar sea,
In harmony's dance, eternally free.
The universe sings of love and dreams,
In rhythmic flow, the cosmos beams.

Celestial Echoes and Soulful Waves

In the stillness of the deep night,
Celestial echoes take their flight.
Waves of wisdom softly crash,
Through the darkness, a gentle splash.

Across the sky, vibrations glow,
Softly revealing what we know.
Stars align in a cosmic trance,
With every pulse, we dare to dance.

In soulful waves, our spirits rise,
Reflections shimmer in the skies.
A tapestry of hope and grace,
In every note, we find our place.

Through endless voids, we journey far,
Guided by each sacred star.
Celestial echoes weave and twine,
In every heart, their light will shine.

So let us sail on waves of light,
Embracing dreams that spark the night.
Celestial whispers call us near,
In the symphony, we disappear.

Pilgrimage Through Stellar Tempests

Across the void, we take our stand,
In stellar tempests, hand in hand.
Guided by the shimmering stars,
We journey forth, no matter how far.

With every storm, a lesson learned,
In cosmic fires, our souls have burned.
Through swirling chaos, winds collide,
We navigate the turning tide.

Bright comets blaze a path anew,
While astral winds call us to pursue.
Amidst the storms, we find our way,
In darkened skies, we seek the day.

Our hearts a compass, strong and true,
In pilgrimage, we gather clues.
Stellar tempests shape our fate,
Through trials faced, we celebrate.

So onward, we tread through space and time,
Each step a story, each breath a rhyme.
In the heart of chaos, we'll reside,
Together forever, side by side.

Murmurs of the Stellar Void

In silence deep, where shadows dwell,
Whispers drift, secrets to tell.
Stars sing soft in cosmic flight,
Echoes lost in the velvet night.

Faint glimmers in the darkened sea,
Spoken dreams of what could be.
Galaxies swirl, a dance so grand,
Each twinkle a wish from distant lands.

Voices of time in stardust thread,
Carried forth, the stories spread.
Murmurs rise from the void so still,
Filling hearts with cosmic thrill.

In this realm where wonders gleam,
We wish upon each fleeting beam.
Infinite tales, we begin to weave,
In the silence, we still believe.

So let us gaze where the shadows play,
Finding hope in the darkened sway.
Murmurs echo, guiding our way,
Through the void, come what may.

Serpents of Light in the Night Sky

Serpents slither through the night,
Dancing softly, pure delight.
Glistening trails in celestial sea,
Guiding travelers, wild and free.

Nebulas breathe, colors intertwine,
With every flicker, stars align.
Twisting like dreams in a silent stream,
Whispers of fate and cosmic theme.

Galactic serpents entwined so tight,
They weave the fabric of our sight.
Flickers of gold, a transient grace,
Painting stories in endless space.

Glimpses of paths that we cannot trace,
In the darkness, we find our place.
Serpent's dance, a guiding thread,
In the firmament, hopes are fed.

As the night wraps us in its shroud,
We stand in awe, humble and proud.
Serpents of light leading the way,
Through the cosmos, we'll find our play.

Beneath the Astral Surface

Beneath the deep where realms reside,
Secrets shimmer, dark and wide.
Rippling waves of time and space,
Whispers gather, lost trails trace.

Hidden worlds lie in embrace,
Each star a story, a cosmic face.
Veils of light, a curtain drawn,
Guard the dreams of dusk till dawn.

In the depths where silence sings,
Celestial songs of ancient things.
Rising tides of thought and lore,
Beneath the surface, yearning more.

Nature's heart beats, soft and low,
Guiding travelers through the flow.
Beneath the astral, truth unfolds,
Timeless wonders, mysteries told.

So dive into the cosmic sea,
Where the heart of the universe can be.
Beneath the astral, we shall roam,
Finding in starlight, a distant home.

Chronicles of the Darkened Firmament

In the firmament, shadows play,
Chronicles of night lead the way.
Stars penned stories in silver bright,
In pages turned by the cloak of night.

Nebulae sigh in colors bold,
Whispers of ancient secrets told.
Time is woven in threads of gray,
Casting shadows upon the day.

Galaxies spiral, tales unwind,
In the darkness, the truth we find.
Lunar echoes, soft and sweet,
Mapping journeys where shadows meet.

The night holds wisdom in every glance,
Inviting dreams to take a chance.
Chronicles written in darkness breathe,
Fueling hopes in every weave.

So gaze upon the midnight skies,
Let the mysteries whisper and rise.
In the firmament, stories bloom,
Chronicles lost in starlight's loom.

Gaze of the Universe in Stillness

In quiet night, the heavens call,
Stars whisper secrets, time stands tall.
Constellations dance, a timeless show,
The vast expanse, a tranquil glow.

Beneath the quiet, our hearts align,
In a fleeting moment, we intertwine.
The universe hums a soothing tune,
As dreams take flight beneath the moon.

Silent reflections on a cosmic sea,
In the stillness, we feel truly free.
Galaxies spin in a lover's embrace,
In this stillness, we find our place.

Time drifts like stardust in the air,
Every moment a glimpse, a prayer.
The world fades, only light remains,
In this gaze, all love sustains.

Eternity wraps us, so divine,
In the gaze of the universe, we shine.
Together we stand, infinite and brave,
In stillness, we find what we crave.

Transient Echoes of the Cosmos

Whispers of light in the cosmic sea,
Fleeting moments, wild and free.
Echoes of stars in a silent shore,
Each pulse a memory, evermore.

We chase the shadows, time will unfold,
Stories of stardust, youthful and bold.
In every heartbeat, the cosmos sighs,
The transient echoes dance in our eyes.

Galaxies swirl in a beautiful spiral,
In the stillness, they speak of survival.
Each flash of light, a tale to tell,
In the transient, we find our well.

Moments as fleeting as the milky way,
Yet they linger on, come what may.
In the vastness, we find our trace,
Transient echoes in boundless space.

Stars may fade, yet they still sing,
In the harmony of everything.
We weave our dreams among the sound,
In transient echoes, love is found.

Celestial Dreams Weaving Tapestries

In the loom of night, dreams entwine,
Stars spin stories, soft and fine.
Patterns of light, threads of grace,
Celestial tapestries in space.

Each wish a stitch, crafted with care,
Woven together, a love laid bare.
Galactic colors, vibrant and bright,
In the tapestry, we find our light.

The cosmos stretches, vast and wide,
In this fabric, we shall abide.
Threads of time twist and bend,
In celestial dreams, there's no end.

With every heartbeat, patterns shift,
In our dreams, we find the gift.
A tapestry woven from dreams and stars,
In the expanse, we heal our scars.

Every twinkling star, a tale unfurled,
A woven memory of the world.
In celestial dreams, we walk in grace,
A tapestry of love we embrace.

Stars as Memories Under the Moon

Under the moon, our wishes gleam,
Stars like memories, a wistful dream.
In the soft light, shadows play,
Moments linger, never stray.

Each star a memory, bright and clear,
Whispers of laughter, moments dear.
In the night sky, our past resides,
Stars as memories, time abides.

The moon watches over, gentle and wise,
As we share our dreams with starry eyes.
Those lights in the sky are never gone,
In the depths of night, they carry on.

Every twinkle paints a story true,
In the silence, we hear what's due.
Stars shine down with a radiant spark,
Memories linger in the dark.

Beneath this sky, we find our tune,
Stars as memories under the moon.
In the night's embrace, our hearts align,
In the glow of love, we forever shine.

Murmurs of Time Beyond the Horizon

Whispers of ages tucked away,
Echoes on the cusp of night.
Shadows dance, soft rays at play,
Emerging dreams, taking flight.

Moments flicker, shades of gray,
As twilight bends the weary seams.
Voices linger, then decay,
Carving paths through silent dreams.

Beyond the veil where starlight glows,
The past entwines with future's call.
In the arc of time, all knowing flows,
Murmurs rise, embracing all.

In gentle waves, the stories weave,
Blind to time, their threads align.
Every heartbeat, joy and grieve,
Across the expanse, eternal design.

Yet still the horizon beckons bright,
A promise in the dusky haze.
With every dawn, a new delight,
The murmurs guide through endless maze.

The Cosmic Tapestry Unraveled

Threads of starlight weave the night,
Patterns old, yet ever new.
Galaxies dance in cosmic flight,
Creating tales in vibrant hue.

Nebulae blossom, colors rare,
Each hue a song from the skies.
Spirals turn in the frozen air,
Unraveling secrets, hidden ties.

Planets spin, in harmony's sway,
A symphony of light and sound.
Boundless wonders beckon to play,
In the vastness, dreams abound.

Comets trace their fleeting arcs,
A moment's glimpse, then gone so fast.
In darkness bright, ignite the sparks,
Through the ages, shadows cast.

The tapestry whispers, soft and clear,
Unveiling visions of what may come.
In every thread, a glimpse so dear,
A cosmic tale, forever spun.

Dark Waters of Celestial Wisdom

In the depths where silence breathes,
Dark waters hold the ancient lore.
Ripples speak of what one believes,
Whispers echo from the shore.

Stars dipped beneath the tranquil wave,
Each shimmer a tale long concealed.
Secrets of the brave and knave,
In darkness, destiny revealed.

The moon reflects its silver truth,
Casting light on what's obscure.
In quiet depths, the key to youth,
Wisdom found, forever pure.

As currents twist and shadows blend,
The mind drifts through the sea of night.
In every bend, a journey's end,
A glimpse of fate in starlit sight.

Drink deep from these celestial tides,
For in the dark, the sage resides.
With every wave, the soul confides,
In dark waters, all wisdom abides.

Harmonies Spun from Celestial Threads

In the loom of night, stars are spun,
Melodies drift through cosmic breeze.
Each whisper creates a world begun,
In perfect tune, nature's tease.

Galactic voices intertwine,
Singing songs of distant lore.
Echoes float on the edge of time,
Building bridges to evermore.

In the silence, hear the hum,
A symphony of light and shade.
Harmony calls, inviting us,
To dance where magic's spun and played.

With every note, the heavens sigh,
Crafting dreams with gentle hands.
Beneath the stars, our spirits fly,
Weaving fate in music's strands.

So close your eyes and drift away,
Into the harmonies that blend.
In celestial threads, we'll sway,
With melodies that never end.

Harmonies of the Starry Abyss

In the night where silence sings,
Whispers of the cosmos cling.
Stars shimmer like ancient dreams,
Through the void, their light redeems.

Galaxies spin in rhythmic dance,
A symphony of fate and chance.
Nebulas bloom, a brilliant hue,
Echoes of wonders, vast and true.

Waves of stardust gently flow,
Across the dark, a cosmic glow.
Each twinkle tells a story old,
Of mysteries in the universe told.

In the vastness, spirits soar,
Beyond the reach of earthly lore.
Harmony in chaos found,
As we drift, unbound, profound.

In this dance of time and space,
We find our essence, our own place.
A serenade of light and dark,
Shining bright, igniting sparks.

Luminous Ripples of Cosmic Yearning

In twilight's embrace, shadows play,
Rippling echoes of dreams sway.
The universe hums a soft tune,
Calling blue and silver moon.

Waves of longing swell and rise,
Crafting tales beneath wide skies.
Celestial dreams in harmony,
Stirring hearts, setting them free.

A tapestry spun with starlit threads,
Where uncharted journeys spread.
In the silence, a spark ignites,
Dancing through the endless nights.

Yearning for realms yet unseen,
Whispers of what might have been.
Each pulse an echo of the past,
In cosmic currents, they are cast.

Through luminous paths, we wander wide,
With stardust dreams as our guide.
Hope glimmers in the vast abyss,
In the void, we seek our bliss.

Constellations of Thought in Cosmic Depths

Thoughts like stars blaze in the night,
Mapping journeys of pure light.
In the cosmos, secrets lie,
Within the depths of a sigh.

Each moment a constellation born,
Across the dark, brightly worn.
We sketch our path in fleeting beams,
Tracing the outline of our dreams.

Ideas swirl like galaxies,
In the vastness, they aim to please.
Galactic navigation of the mind,
Finding treasures, slow but kind.

In every thought, a spark of gold,
A tapestry of stories told.
Whispered truths in cosmic flow,
Unraveling what we yearn to know.

Beneath the stars, our hearts align,
In the infinite, we intertwine.
Exploring depths of vast unknown,
In the void, our essence grown.

The Vortices of Memory and Infinity

In the whirl of time's embrace,
Memories linger, leaving trace.
Vortices twist, pulling near,
Echoes of laughter, love, and fear.

Each moment a spiral, round and round,
Capturing whispers, lost and found.
In the dance of what has been,
Infinity calls us to its sheen.

Thoughts like tendrils reach and weave,
Through the fabric of what we believe.
In fleeting glimpses, we reside,
Within the current of the tide.

Waves of time crash on the shore,
A timeless song forevermore.
As we navigate the unknown sea,
The vortices guide us, wild and free.

In this cycle of ebb and flow,
We find our way, we come to know.
Memory dances with infinity's grace,
In the vastness, we find our place.

The Heartbeat of Forgotten Galaxies

In shadows where the stardust lies,
Whispers of ancient dreams arise.
Faint echoes of a time long past,
In silence, their memories cast.

Galaxies drift in a quiet dance,
Each twinkle holds a secret chance.
Lightyears away, tales yet untold,
In the dark, their wonders unfold.

Through the void where silence reigns,
A heartbeat pulses through the plains.
With every throb, worlds intertwine,
Lost in space, yet so divine.

Forgotten are the voices clear,
Yet in the cosmos, they remain near.
In the stillness, one can feel,
The heartbeat that time cannot conceal.

Echoing Lullabies on the Cosmic Breeze

A gentle sigh of night unfolds,
Cradling dreams in hues of gold.
Whispers drift on stardust trails,
Where every wish and hope prevails.

Lullabies sung by the celestial choir,
Wrapped in warmth, lifting us higher.
Echoes soft like a feathered touch,
In the cosmic vastness, we feel so much.

Stars blink like notes in a tranquil song,
Carried on winds that flow along.
Each note a promise softly shared,
In the universe's arms, we are bared.

As night wraps us in its dark embrace,
Lullabies weave through time and space.
In the quiet, our spirits rise,
Glimmers of hope in twilight skies.

Beneath the Twilight's Glistening Veil

Beneath the veil where twilight gleams,
A tapestry of woven dreams.
Stars ignite in the fading light,
Whispering secrets of the night.

The horizon blushes soft and shy,
Birds sing as the day waves goodbye.
Colors blend in a painter's grace,
Nature's beauty fills this space.

In the stillness, horizons shift,
Silent moments become a gift.
Every shadow begins to sway,
As the night prepares for play.

Underneath the shimmering hue,
Magic whispers, pure and true.
Beneath the twilight's watchful eye,
Our hopes ascend, and dreams will fly.

The Stillness Between Celestial Waves

In the hush between the stars' embrace,
Lies a world, a timeless space.
Celestial waves, they rise and fall,
Cradling dreams and silent calls.

In the space where shadows merge,
Tranquility begins to surge.
Each ripple sings in subtle tones,
A universe that feels like home.

Floating softly, we drift along,
Held by the universe's song.
In the pause, the heart takes flight,
Navigating through the night.

Every breath a cosmic dance,
In the stillness, we find our chance.
Between the waves, our spirits soar,
In the void, we seek for more.

Interstellar Whispers in Night's Clutch

In the dark, where shadows play,
Whispers float and drift away.
Stars weave tales with silver thread,
Guiding dreams of those who tread.

Galaxies twirl in silent dance,
Filling hearts with cosmic chance.
Every glimmer, a story spun,
A timeless bond, two worlds as one.

Through the void, a soft embrace,
Echoes linger, find their place.
In night's clutch, we lose our fears,
As starlit paths draw us near.

Celestial maps traced in light,
Navigating through the night.
Eclipsed by shadows, we ignite,
A spark of hope, our burning sight.

Interstellar dreams take flight,
Together, finding cosmic height.
In endless space, we share our sighs,
Beneath the grand, eternal skies.

The Silence of Stars and Time's Secrets

In the quiet, stars unveil,
Whispers soft, like a gentle sail.
Time sways softly, an endless stream,
Holding secrets in its gleam.

Every twinkle, a promise made,
In the shadow of the glade.
Moments frozen, lost in flight,
The silence sings, a pure delight.

Memories etched in cosmic dust,
In this stillness, we find trust.
A heartbeat echoing in space,
Time's embrace, an endless chase.

Galaxies blend in a hush,
While dreams around, like rivers rush.
In the vastness, serenity reigns,
As the cosmos whispers its refrains.

Through the veil of night, we roam,
Among the stars, we find our home.
In time's secrets, we ignite,
Together, shining through the night.

Celestial Refractions in the Soul's Mirror

Refractions dance in twilight's hue,
Mirrors reflect the cosmos too.
The soul expands with every glance,
In this realm, we find our chance.

Galactic laughter fills the air,
Starlit dreams, we gladly share.
Each vision rich with color bright,
We embrace the depths of night.

Through astral windows, light cascades,
In the stillness, serenity wades.
Consciousness blooms like nebulae,
In the mirror, we dare to fly.

Celestial echoes hum and sway,
Guiding our thoughts, showing the way.
Infinite paths stretch out ahead,
In the universe, we're led.

With every breath, we intertwine,
Reflections spark, our hearts align.
In constellations, truth is found,
In both silence and sound.

Eclipsed Dreams of Wanderers

In the dusk where shadows dwell,
Dreamers roam, casting their spell.
Eclipsed visions, bold and bright,
Stir the heart, ignite the night.

Wanderers seek the cosmic light,
Chasing whispers, taking flight.
With every step, a story unfolds,
In the fabric of the stars, we hold.

The moon dances, a guiding glow,
In secrets wrapped, we come to know.
Each heartbeat syncs with the tide,
Through the dark, we boldly glide.

Eclipsed dreams unveil our fate,
Threads of destiny intertwine and create.
As night deepens, we find our way,
In stardust songs, we choose to stay.

Together we drift, as wanderers do,
In the vast unknown, our spirits grew.
Under the veil, of endless skies,
In eclipsed dreams, our hearts will rise.

Echoes of Starlit Waters

Ripples form where silence dwells,
Beneath the moon, the water swells.
Stars reflected, a glimmering dance,
A tranquil night, lost in a trance.

Gentle whispers from depths below,
The heart of night begins to glow.
Dreams afloat on the mirror's face,
In starlit waters, we find our place.

Flickering lights in the velvet sea,
Waves of calm: a symphony.
Each echo sings of tales long gone,
Where time stands still, and hope is drawn.

Secrets linger in the air,
Floating softly, without a care.
Embrace the night, let worries fade,
In echoes sweet, memories are made.

Beneath the stars, our spirits soar,
Hand in hand, we search for more.
In every ripple, every sway,
Echoes call as night turns day.

Whispers Beneath the Cosmic Veil

Softly spoken, the cosmos sighs,
Underneath myriad endless skies.
Mysteries weave in the threads of night,
Veiled in stardust, shimmering light.

Galaxies spin, secrets unfold,
In whispers soft, the universe told.
Celestial tales in the lunar glow,
A dance of shadows in ebb and flow.

Eternity breathes in twilight's fold,
With every star, a story bold.
Whispers rise from the cosmic sea,
Unravel the dreams that yearn to be.

Veils of time drift and glide,
Within the silence, hope abides.
As echoes of starlight kiss the dawn,
Under the heavens, we dream on and on.

Beneath the veil, our spirits bond,
In cosmic whispers, we respond.
Listen closely, let your heart feel,
The gentle words that time will reveal.

Dreams Adrift in the Infinite Sky

Floating softly on clouds of grace,
In the vast expanse, we find our place.
Dreams take flight on the wings of night,
Drifting freely, a serene sight.

Stars twinkle like thoughts unspoken,
In the infinite sky, hearts awaken.
Each aspiration, a comet's tail,
A journey begun, where we set sail.

Weightless visions, a canvas wide,
Carry our hopes on the evening tide.
As stardust weaves through the cosmic sea,
We wander boldly, forever free.

Beneath constellations, love will guide,
Warmed by the glow of fate's sweet tide.
With every breath, a new dream's born,
As dawn approaches, we're gently sworn.

Adrift in the sky, let souls combine,
In the vastness, our spirits shine.
With every heartbeat, let dreams ignite,
In the infinite, we find our light.

Shadows Danced by Astral Light

In the stillness, shadows play,
Beneath the moon's soft, glowing ray.
Whispers of night, a soothing tune,
As dark entwines with the silver moon.

Figures twirl in the cosmic glow,
Time stands still as secrets flow.
A ballet of light in the velvet night,
Our souls entwined, oh what a sight!

Echoes shimmer on the edge of dawn,
Where shadows linger, we are drawn.
With every step in celestial space,
Our hearts beat to the universe's pace.

Dancing softly, our spirits soar,
In astral light, we seek for more.
The night embraces, with magic rife,
In shadows danced, we find our life.

As dawn awakens the dreams we've spun,
The performance ends, but we have won.
With visions clear and hearts so bright,
We carry forth the astral light.

Ethereal Journeys through Silent Night

Under the veil of whispered dreams,
Stars glimmer softly, like silver beams.
The moon cradles secrets, old and bright,
Guiding our hearts through the silent night.

Footsteps echo on paths unseen,
Awakening wonders, where we have been.
In shadows, the whispers of time unfold,
Tales of the beauty, both fragile and bold.

Winds rustle gently, carrying thought,
To places where solace can be sought.
Each breath a promise, a moment reclaimed,
In the quiet embrace, we are unchained.

Constellations weave through the velvet sky,
A tapestry rich, where our spirits fly.
With every heartbeat, we dance and we sway,
In the presence of night, we find our way.

Ethereal journeys shimmer with grace,
Guided by love, in this sacred space.
As dawn gently breaks, and shadows take flight,
We carry the magic of the silent night.

Celestial Mosaics of Forgotten Dreams

In the depths of slumber, dreams take flight,
Patterns of starlight, hidden from sight.
Each memory sparkles, a bead of delight,
Woven together in the fabric of night.

Fragments of laughter and whispers of hopes,
Dance through the cosmos, like intricate ropes.
They merge and they shift, like waves on the stream,
Creating mosaics, our flickering dream.

In stillness, we hear the soft echoes call,
Of adventures uncharted, of rise and fall.
Through the lens of the heart, we glimpse and we see,
How fragile and fierce our dreams can be.

Celestial sparkles dust the sky wide,
Holding the stories with love as a guide.
Though time may erase, and horizons may change,
These mosaics remain, vibrant and strange.

As we wake from the night, let us not forget,
The dreams that we cherished, the paths we have met.
In the dance of the stars, may we always believe,
In the power of dreaming, in all we achieve.

Dance of Shadows in the Starry Field

Beneath the expanse where the wild stars play,
Shadows are stretching, in the cool evening sway.
They flicker and twirl in a rhythm so fine,
A silent ballet through the soft pines.

Moonlight drapes softly on faces aglow,
As starlit whispers begin to flow.
The night weaves a spell, dark yet divine,
In this quiet dance, our spirits entwine.

Glimmers of hope flare in the night air,
While shadows embrace, without any care.
Each figure takes shape, then fades into dreams,
In a world where nothing is ever as it seems.

The heartbeat of night resonates deep,
In the rhythm of shadows, where secrets can keep.
Together we sway, as awe fills the field,
In the dance of the stars, our hearts are revealed.

As dawn approaches, and shadows retreat,
The lessons we learned will never taste sweet.
Yet echoes of laughter will linger and bind,
In the dance of the shadows, what treasures we find.

Crystalline Gazes into the Vast Unknown

With crystalline gazes, we search the expanse,
The vast unknown sings, beckoning us to dance.
Each twinkle a promise, each glimmer a chance,
To uncover the wonders of life's grand romance.

In the silence of starlight, truth starts to bloom,
Illuminating paths where shadows loom.
The heart's gentle whispers pour into the night,
As we step into magic, towards the light.

Voices of galaxies brush close like a sigh,
In the depths of our being, we reach for the sky.
Through crystalline visions, our hopes intertwine,
Stargazing seekers, destinies align.

Each shimmering facet reflects what we seek,
In the dance of the cosmos, where bonds are unique.
We rise on the currents, embracing the glide,
In the depths of the vastness, where dreams coincide.

With crystalline gazes, we forge our own fate,
Exploring the wonders that patiently wait.
In the heart of the night, let our spirits unfurl,
As we delve into depths of a shimmering world.

Songs of the Void and Vibrant Stars

In the silence, whispers call,
Echos dance through space's thrall.
Shadows play in endless night,
Stars ignite with flickering light.

Galaxies spin in cosmic grace,
Timeless tales in vast embrace.
Each pulse, a note in dark's refrain,
Songs of the void, where dreams remain.

Nebulas bloom in colors rare,
Infinite wonders weave through air.
In this realm, the heart beats strong,
Vibrant stars sing their ancient song.

Thoughts travel on celestial streams,
In the cosmos, weave our dreams.
In the dance of atoms, we grow,
The fabric of space begins to flow.

In the black, we find our light,
Guided by the stars so bright.
Their tales of old, they gently share,
Beneath the void, all is laid bare.

Forever echoing in time's face,
Songs that drift through endless space.
In shadows deep, new worlds aspire,
In vibrant songs, we never tire.

Silent Scenes Beneath the Astral Canopy

Underneath the starry domes,
Silent scenes of cosmic homes.
Whispers float on gentle breezes,
In this realm, the heart eases.

Galaxies paint with silver ink,
Time dissolves, we pause and think.
Every flicker, a tale untold,
In the vast, a warmth to behold.

Stardust weaves through dreams we chase,
In the shadows, we find our place.
Moonbeams dance on quiet shores,
While silence speaks of distant wars.

Beneath the veil of night's embrace,
Hidden stories thrumming in space.
Constellations map our fears,
In their glow, we shed our tears.

The universe breathes, calm and wide,
Silent scenes where mysteries bide.
Stars above, like lanterns burn,
In their light, our souls will turn.

Through the stillness, hope takes flight,
In the dark, we cling to light.
With every pulse, we come to see,
Silent scenes are part of we.

Astral Dreams Woven in Twilight

As twilight falls, the stars align,
In astral dreams, our hearts entwine.
Colors fade in dusk's warm glow,
Bringing forth a cosmic flow.

Woven threads of night's embrace,
Time unravels in this space.
Celestial whispers, soft and bright,
Guide us through the velvet night.

Floating softly on twilight's breeze,
In the dark, our spirits ease.
Hopes emerge like fireflies,
Dancing gently through the skies.

Stars ignite with silver threads,
In astral dreams, the wisdom spreads.
Weaving tales of old and new,
In their light, we find what's true.

The cosmos hums a lullaby,
As galaxies swirl and fly.
In this dream, we find our call,
Twilight's beauty holds us all.

With hearts aglow, we reach to find,
Connected threads of every kind.
In the starlight, we will stay,
Woven dreams that never fray.

Visions Lost in the Cosmic Flow

In the depths of space, we drift,
Visions lost in cosmic rift.
Time slips through our grasping hands,
As we wander through the lands.

Nebulas swirl, colors collide,
In the night, our thoughts reside.
Whispers echo in the dark,
Lighting up a single spark.

Galactic rivers twist and turn,
In the currents, we discern.
Each moment holds a fleeting glance,
In the void, we find our chance.

Echoes of the past arise,
Bringing forth forgotten ties.
In the flow, we start to see,
Visions dance, wild and free.

Time and space begin to weave,
In this cosmos, we believe.
All that once was, comes alive,
Lost in flow, we will survive.

In the vastness, we are whole,
In the silence, find our soul.
Through the cosmic sea we roam,
In lost visions, we find home.

Secrets of the Etherial Rift

Whispers flow through starlit skies,
Mysteries in silence lie.
The rift sings a haunting tune,
Beneath the glowing crescent moon.

Fragments of dreams drift afar,
Echoes of a fallen star.
In shadows deep, truths await,
Guided by the hands of fate.

Celestial dance unfolds in flight,
Veils are lifted in the night.
With every pulse, new worlds align,
In the void, existence entwines.

Threads of time weave through the dark,
Carving paths to leave a mark.
The rift, a gateway unexplored,
Where endless wonders are stored.

Secrets beckon, soft and bright,
In the ether, pure delight.
Journey forth with heart ablaze,
Through cosmic mazes, lost in haze.

Navigating the Cosmic Reflection

Mirrors of the universe gleam,
Reflecting every hidden dream.
Stars align in rhythmic dance,
Guiding hearts through endless chance.

Galaxies spin, a tapestry wide,
In their depths, mysteries abide.
We sail on ships of light and sound,
In the cosmos, freedom found.

Waves of time whisper in the void,
Paths we walk, both loved and coyed.
Every choice a ripple makes,
In the fabric, destiny breaks.

Celestial charts drawn with care,
Navigating through the cosmic air.
With every pulse, the heart ignites,
In wonder of the starry nights.

Reflections shimmer, truth revealed,
In the cosmic, wounds are healed.
As we journey, hand in hand,
Through the universe, vast and grand.

Dances of Nebulae and Echoes

Nebulae bloom in colors bright,
Dancing softly, pure delight.
Stars are born within their folds,
Tales of ages, yet untold.

In the silence, echoes play,
Melodies from faraway.
With every pulse, the cosmos sways,
In the dark, a gentle blaze.

Winds of change sweep through the space,
Carving whispers, leaving grace.
In the whirl, creation spins,
From chaos, comfort begins.

Eternal waltz of time and light,
Shadows dance in the quiet night.
Nebulae weave their glowing seams,
Binding together our shared dreams.

In the tapestry of the expanse,
Every star finds its own chance.
Together we twirl in the grand ballet,
As echoes of the past softly sway.

Songs of the Unseen Universe

Voices call from realms unknown,
In the silence, seeds are sown.
The universe hums a tune,
Written in the light of the moon.

Harmony flows through the dark,
Drawing forth each hidden spark.
With every note, the stars align,
Creating chords, so divine.

Melodies from the heart of space,
Resonate in time and place.
Every being sings their part,
In the symphony of the heart.

Unseen wonders, soft and clear,
Echoes of love we hold dear.
As we sing through the astral sea,
Finding truth in unity.

Together we rise, side by side,
In the cosmic dance, we abide.
The unseen universe sings aloud,
In the silence, we're unbowed.

Echoing Dreams in Cosmic Depths

In the silence of the night,
Whispers dance like fireflies.
Thoughts drift on the cosmic wind,
Carried far beyond the skies.

Stars hum tunes from ages past,
Melodies of ancient lore.
Galaxies spin in harmony,
Echoes calling evermore.

Beyond the veil, dreams awaken,
Vibrant colors swirl and spark.
In the heart of darkness glisten,
Light ignites the hidden arc.

Time collapses, moments blend,
A tapestry of stardust spun.
In the depths where shadows bide,
We find the threads that weave as one.

Here we drift, a cosmic dance,
Lost in thoughts that ebb and flow.
In the echoes of our dreams,
Infinite wonders start to grow.

Beneath the Surface of the Universe

Beneath the vast and starlit skies,
Lies a world we cannot see.
In shadows deep, the secrets dwell,
Whispers of eternity.

Galaxies pulse with hidden light,
Planets spin in silent grace.
A tapestry of life unfolds,
In every crevice, every space.

The silence speaks of ancient waves,
Time's embrace, a gentle tide.
Memories of the cosmic birth,
In the depths where dreams reside.

Comets trail their silver paths,
Across the heavens, stories weave.
In the stillness, wisdom flows,
From the cosmos, we believe.

So let us dive into the night,
Where wonders linger, unexplored.
Beneath the surface, life abounds,
In the silent song, restored.

Celestial Choir of Forgotten Realms

In the twilight of forgotten dreams,
A choir sings of worlds unknown.
Voices rise like gentle winds,
Carrying tales from the stone.

Echoes of laughter brush the stars,
Where shadows dance in twilight's breath.
Somewhere lost in cosmic time,
They sing of life, they sing of death.

Harmony in the vast abyss,
Waves of sound in endless sea.
Each note a spark of distant light,
Calling forth what's meant to be.

Reverberations of ancient hearts,
Beat in rhythm with the night.
In the stillness, whispers meld,
Creating visions pure and bright.

Celestial choirs weave their dreams,
A tapestry of sights unseen.
Together in the cosmic sway,
Forever bound in love's serene.

Starlight's Lament in Stillness

Beneath the crescent moon's soft glow,
A longing stirs within the night.
Stars above, they softly weep,
Pouring sorrow, pure and bright.

In the quiet, echoes linger,
Carried on the whispering breeze.
Each twinkle tells a story lost,
Of dreams entwined among the trees.

The universe breathes in silence,
Moonbeams cast their silver sigh.
In the stillness, hearts awaken,
To the lullaby that flows high.

Fleeting moments slip like sand,
Through the hourglass of our fate.
In starlight's embrace we find peace,
While time weaves love, while time waits.

Yet shadows softly mark the path,
Of beauty tinged with gentle pain.
In the lament of starlit dreams,
We find our joy amidst the rain.

Unraveled Dreams in Celestial Currents

In the fabric of night, whispers glide,
Stars beckon softly, secrets provided.
Threads of silver weave through the dark,
Where dreams unravel, igniting a spark.

Galaxies dance in a silk-spun grace,
Echoes of wishes drift through space.
Beneath the glow of ethereal lights,
Hope takes flight on celestial nights.

Tidal waves of thought crash on the shore,
Carried on winds, forever to soar.
Eclipsed by longing, the cosmos sighs,
As lovers entwine beneath far-off skies.

Nebulae cradle each breath we take,
In cosmic embrace, our hearts awake.
Colors collide in a mystical swirl,
Transcending the bounds of this earthly world.

With every heartbeat, the universe spins,
Unraveled dreams, where the journey begins.
Across constellations, we wander and roam,
In the vastness above, we find our home.

The Depths of Stars and Silence

In silence profound, the stars softly glow,
Whispers of cosmos in shadows below.
Each twinkle a story, a fable untold,
In the depths of the night, secrets unfold.

Galactic winds hush the cries of the past,
Echoes of eternity, overlaid and vast.
Gravity pulls at the heart of the void,
While the silence of stars keeps our dreams buoyed.

Through the veil of time, where mysteries meet,
The depths of existence pulse beneath our feet.
Stars murmur softly, lost in their trance,
Guiding the way with a cosmic romance.

Infinite layers of dark intertwine,
In the quiet of space, we search for the sign.
The dance of the stars, a delicate grace,
In the depths of silence, we find our place.

As light years stretch from the heart of our gaze,
We wander alone through the nebulous haze.
Yet in the stillness, the cosmos thrives,
In the depths of stars, our spirit survives.

Visions Cast in Cosmic Realms

In realms of the cosmos, visions take flight,
Painted by starlight, dreams burn so bright.
Vistas of wonder, swirling and grand,
Each thought a spark from a guiding hand.

Nebulas whisper their tales of the past,
Time flows like rivers, steady and fast.
Cosmic horizons stretch far and wide,
Boundless the journey, let fate be our guide.

In the tapestry woven of dark and of light,
Visions entwine in a dance of the night.
From black holes to comets, the stories arise,
In cosmic embrace, we learn to be wise.

Beyond the horizon, the unknown calls clear,
Chasing the stars, we conquer our fear.
With each passing moment, new worlds we find,
In visions of space, we expand our mind.

Journey with me through this infinite sea,
Together we'll wander, forever be free.
In cosmic realms where the heartbeats align,
We'll cast our own fate in the stars that shine.

Starlight Dreams in the Abyss's Embrace

In the abyss deep, where shadows entwine,
Starlight dreams shimmer, sparkles divine.
Wrapped in a silence, soft as a sigh,
We dance with our visions, as comets fly by.

Embraced by the night, our spirits will soar,
Into the unknown, forever explore.
Galaxies twinkle in the depths of despair,
Yet starlight dreams bring hope to the air.

In the cradle of darkness, we weave our fate,
Twinkling desires that patiently wait.
Beneath the vast canvas, painted in hues,
Our dreams come alive in the night's gentle muse.

Each heartbeat echoes through the cavernous deep,
Murmurs of wishes that promise to keep.
In the abyss's embrace, where wonders reside,
We uncover the magic that darkness can hide.

Under the watch of the moon's silver gaze,
Starlight dreams beckon through mystical ways.
In shadows we linger, our hopes interlace,
In the depths of the night, we find our grace.